To Jim

CAPE TOWN STATION
A POETIC JOURNEY FROM
CAPE TOWN TO KANSAS

GLORIA CREED-DIKEOGU

With Best Wishes Gloria Creed-Dikeogu

DEDICATION

I dedicate these poems to my husband Nathaniel Dikeogu, my son Chijike Dikeogu, to the members of the De Kock and Creed Families for whom I have the greatest love and respect. In loving memory of my parents Henry and Kathleen Creed, and my cousin, Grant Hankey. Thank You for the memories, for your caring and the inspiration.

CONTENTS

Awakening	1
Secret Cave	2
You	3
Longing	4
Dreams	6
A Parting Gift	8
Diepriver Station	9
Battle of Wills	13
Daughter of Africa	14
Heathfield Station	16
Just Wishing	20
Guilt Echo	21
Reaction to the Death of an Old Friend	22
Forgiveness on the Death of an Old Friend	24
Hold me	26
Insecurity	27
Tomorrow	28
Protest	29
Thoughts in parting	30
Realization	32
Lament for an almost lost love	33

Houston 35

Body of Bronze 37

Process of Analysis: A Poem dedicated to the Sisterhood of 38
Zeta Phi Beta Sorority, Omega Theta Chapter

Colliding Worlds 39

My inspiration 41

Cramming 42

I wonder why 44

The photograph 45

The Bubble Burst 46

Unity in differentness 48

Autumn anger 49

How can you joke? 51

Weaknesses 52

Teddy Bear 54

Defining my world 56

The Visitor 58

Questioning life 60

The Puzzle 62

Complain 64

Masquerade 66

All I have wanted 68

Despair 69

Modern Sonnet to an Unborn Child   71

Essence of Life   72

Lightening   74

A message for the baby   75

To the little one   76

What is that sound I hear?   78

The way of life   80

Pacified   82

Sleep little one   84

Thoughts in returning   86

The Climb   88

Cape Town Station   90

Behind Mowbray Station   92

Shock redefined: On the death of a family member   95

Portrait of Eternal Youth   98

The chain is forever broken   100

Life is like a train   102

About the Author   107

Awakening

My muse has awakened
From a long gentle sleep
And beckons me come,
A new watch to keep.

To deepen my musings
And strengthen my pen
To sharpen understanding
Write much more than then.

I know I am ready
Experience is ripe
So much still must happen
Smoke curls from my pipe.

So come now fair muse
Come teach me anew
And I will sing well
And sing strong and sing true.

SECRET CAVE

My heart is like a secret cave
    Bejeweled with the
        Stalactites and stalactites
            of lived experiences.

YOU

Are you really all I see
Or are you more?
The snow falls like a ghostly sheet
Creeping in on the land
On my house.
    Grey skies threaten
    But I do not fear
    I am secure
    Yet the cold envelopes me and my heart
Enfolding us,
Closing us in.
    But then there's you.
Gentle and warm in my mid
Melting the cold—
Starting the fire that melts and molds and rages
Tending it,
Fueling it,
Until it grows, grey-red-hot flames
Consuming all.

LONGING

I twist and turn,

Restless in the night.

Touching the pillows of my bed,

But you're not there.

I turn over again

To look at the clock

And say your name out loud

Hoping you will hear me.

But will you?

Could you?

You're so far away—

In another house

In another world

In another bed

And I try to understand

Why it is that you are there

When you should be here,

With me.

DREAMS

You turn and walk away

Her hand in your hand.

She smiles

But you do not.

Her face is clear, familiar,

But yours is unclear, but loved.

A cry escapes me

Filling the dark room with haunting echoes

Of the past

My heart is a heavy-empty-leaden casket

For I cannot hide the insecurities

that haunt and threaten to defeat.

Why do they persist to confront me.

Face to face—

Even in my dreams?

A PARTING GIFT

I will not part from you,

But if I must,

And have no choice,

Then sow the seed,

So I may raise

The good corn as a legacy

And eat it

For the rest of my life.

DIEPRIVER STATION

Solitary-loneliness descends on me

disembarking from the train

At Diepriver Station.

In the late afternoon.

I do not know the faces that were so loved

Long ago when life was good

And parents plenty.

But now

No-one follows

As on exit

It is an almighty climb

Up steep grey stairs

one step at a time

Heavy shopping bags

Overbalancing—

As the ascent is made

To the uppermost reaches of the bridge.

Cognizant of every footfall,

Every noise

Every voice on the wind

I walk on

Let the cars pass

In silent mockery.

A woman towers over me---

Her shadow, long and narrow crosses mine

As I find a balance

Between my bags,

And with a heavy-checkered-blanketed pinned front

She ventures ever closer

Her footsteps, heavy-uneven

On the shadowy pavement.

She carries a child on her back and

A fat bundle on her head

Her arms swing to and fro

And then up to her head

To steady her bundle.

Looking down on approach

She barely misses

Knocking into me

As we overcrowd the sidewalk.

But we pass each other

Without a word

Without a greeting

Without a backward glance,

Continuing on

In opposite directions that coincide for a split second

And on toward lives filled with different-similarities.

And as the afternoon turns into evening

I cross the second bridge

Into Punts Estate

The yellow sun, glittering at my back

And the shadows fast-deeping on our uncertain future.

BATTLE OF WILLS

I fight for control

But you will not let me be the controller.

It's a battle of wills.

My will

Against Yours.

You make your strength felt,

Over and over,

Again and Again,

Like Hercules taming Aphrodite.

DAUGHTER OF AFRICA

Africa is far-off

but I still see Africa in my dreams,

speak my language

in my mind when I'm thinking,

call on my ancestors

when I'm speaking to God,

dance and sing like my people do

when I'm satisfied with life,

cook as I have learnt to do

as my mother and her mother taught,

held on to my traditions

as I did in my youth.

Yes, Africa is far-off

But I still live and relive

Africa every day.

HEATHFIELD STATION

Late for school again

    Are you?

That you must go

    Just one station!

Could you not walk?

Memories

    Visual replays

    Daily

Of countless days gone by.

How well I still remember

    When I was just a girl

And life was made of endless

School mishaps

Train-trips

New clothes

Hairdresser appointments

New shoes

Birthday celebrations

Lively family dinners

Laughter

Togetherness

Bad TV-dubbing...

Ah yes, I remember her voice,

As if it were yesterday,

Coming to me

Like an echo

Through those loving years.

Faces will fade—

Pictures will tarnish,

Yet year by year

I relive those yesterdays

17

As if I was with her

As if she was here

And we were still close;

For it was just yesterday

When I held her hand

Kissed her cheek

Touched her face

And called her "Mum"

When I'm heavy in heart

And so cold and alone

And I long for her wisdom

And her gentle firm tone

Then I close my eyes

And I open my heart

And it feels then as if

We are never to part

For I know that she breathes

In my mind and my soul

And her counsel and kindness

Forever makes me whole.

JUST WISHING

Blow out the candles

And make a wish.

Do you wish for a

Cardboard future

Full of paper jets

And paper dreams?

Or do you need a quarter

For a wishing-well?

GUILT ECHO

I can't change the past

And I can't turn the clock back

Yet I wish I could…I wish I could.

But I can change the present

And I can make life livable

I'm sure I could…I'm sure I could…

And I sure I could…Am I sure I could…?

REACTION TO THE DEATH OF AN OLD FRIEND

They told me

And I can't forget

How you met your fate.

Unforeseen—

So bizarre,

Too macabre,

When the train pulled into the station

And you clambered on.

Who would have thought

There would come a day

When you'd slip-fall

Between train and platform

And be dragged

Clothing trapped,

Platform length—

Within inches of death.

Great God—

You judge us both,

Our dire infractions weigh—

But in your mercy

We are dust

And into dust relay.

FORGIVENESS ON THE DEATH OF AN OLD FRIEND

The years have fled

And yet—

   You asked for forgiveness

     And it was so hard—

       Unbearable,

         Hurtful—

But I forgave you

    With a heavy-leaden heart

As you lay supine

On your sick-bed

   Legless,

   Train-crash-mangled-disfigured

   Life, ebbing away.

Now you're gone

     God alone knows

     Whose fault it was

         All those years ago,

            When you and I

               Chose to tangle

Disarrange

     Corrupt

     Everyone's lives

         Through our unforgivable conduct of disgrace.

HOLD ME

Touch me for I want

Your wisdom to caress

My mind.

Hold me for when you

Hold my heart

You empower my soul.

INSECURITY

She lusts for you

And I love you

She'll play her game

And you'll play her game

Then she'll win you

But I love you.

She'll trap you

And I love you

She'll bed you

And I love you

And I'll lose you

To her lust.

TOMORROW

Oh yes, tomorrow will come and go;

And we will be together again,

Like two peas in a pod

Two fish in the sea,

Swimming side by side,

Wet and happy.

And what will tomorrow bring?

Today I cannot tell—

The calm before the storm?

PROTEST

Yes, you bore me

But I am born to a will,

A choice between life and death

And how to live and let live

I have become

And am as I am

Through pain and joy, pain and sorrow,

Laughter and happiness,

Success and defeat

And my chosen path leads to the future.

And I choose to live it well.

THOUGHTS IN PARTING

Are we to part,

You and I,

With just a plain goodbye—

After all we've had

And all we've been through together?

No—

It is too hard—

You cannot run away

And shirk your responsibilities—

We must face the future

And the uncertainties that loom, enlarged—

For like the birds,

We must feather our nest,

And be ready together,

When Spring comes.

REALIZATION

It's a simple-complexity.

Bits and pieces

Fit together in my mind—

And as I get ready to go out alone--

And see what the outside world has to offer—

I realize that some of the pieces

Are there already

For I have

My gifts,

    My weapons of self-defense

      My past

      My future

And what self can ultimately make of self.

LAMENT FOR AN ALMOST LOST LOVE

We love each other

You and I

But do we have a future?

For I must return to the Motherland soon,

And I will be alone without you.

You will be here

And I will be there

We will be separated,

Alone without each other.

I cannot stay,

For I do not belong where you do

And you do not belong where I do.

So what about our future now?

What will we do?

What will you do?

Will you forget me so easily,

And carry on with life?

Will you say goodbye

And forget in another girl's arms?

Will you bid farewell

After all we've been through

And all we've had together?

Or will you fight as one with me to be...

Here together,

To be together legally,

I am fighting...but are you?

HOUSTON

Soon you will fly towards the sunshine

Free of a society of ice

That sheltered and imprisoned you

Tradition and culture beckons

And you cannot disobey the call

Miles lay between here and home,

Yet you are ready to discuss new ideas,

Willing to meet challenges of a new day,

Excited to hear a tongue you've used before

To sing praise and argue points.

Bracing yourself to deliver blows of knowledge

And wisdom and be a contender in the fight

For power and wealth in this, great big world.

But you're no ordinary contender

For you stand alone against the world

Unique and Universal

Transcending all.

BODY OF BRONZE

I cannot tear my eyes away,

For you are shaped

And chiseled by the master's hand

With perfection and humanity,

A hard and delicate statute—

Made of the same precious metals

That mold the mind.

PROCESS OF ANALYSIS:
A POEM DEDICATED TO THE SISTERHOOD OF
ZETA PHI BETA SORORITY, OMEGA THETA CHAPTER

Delicate white petals are closed

Light dew drops

    Assemble on them,

        And slowly dry.

As it becomes morning

    As it becomes warmer,

        The petal slit is open

        To the gentleness of sunbeams

            Then two transparent dew drops

            Are newly added,

            And as the petals completely open

            To the bright sunshine

The dew drops fall into the Central flower.

COLLIDING WORLDS

I see you in my mind's eye

On the couch

Comfortable, yet deep in thought,

Contemplating the problems of life

And trying to find solutions.

I can't predict future happenings but

The suspense is

Somewhat fulfilling for us both.

For there is promise of a future,

Yet right now it's hard to make ends meet.

I didn't belong to your world but

Now that I do

Now that our worlds collide-spilling-over

We are working at the

Challenge of each new day

Separately-but-together.

We are separate

And yet together

You and I.

Two seeds in the same ground

Watered by the gardener,

Maturing and flowering side-by-side.

MY INSPIRATION

I was a mirage in the desert of life,

Where travelers longed to drink, but died of thirst

Or choked in the mud in the middle of a no-man's land,

Where no trees could ever flourish.

But now my oasis is beautiful and green,

And I am a deepening well,

Filled with bountiful, life-giving water

From which many will want to drink.

My waters are wholesome and sweet

Since they have been dug and replenished

By your resilient stream.

CRAMMING

Can't remember head from tail

What I learnt—

Rearing to go

And try to do my best—

With a mind full of what-ifs, what-nows,

And mushed up information.

And I need to reorganize everything—

Everything, from back to front and front to back.

But—No—No,

Now Nothing No longer makes sense,

No matter!

Great God in me,

Grant me wisdom in the midst this mindless confusion.

I WONDER WHY

The rain falls at my window

I hear its nosy patter.

Its big drops fall to the ground

And the anger of the wind increase

As the raindrops are directed at me and at my window.

And I wonder why I it that sometimes

    My tears fall like the rain outside

    My emotions rage like the increasing anger of the storm

    My mood matches the cold-gray of the skies outside

But when you are there

    The sun shines again in my heart.

THE PHOTOGRAPH

I remember the times when we were all together.

When times were better,

When people were younger,

And everything was simpler.

But now, so much has changed—

Years go by,

People change,

Family ties weaken,

Others strengthen,

Children grow.

So we hold onto the memories we have of yesterday

And try to redirect tomorrow.

THE BUBBLE BURST

The bubble burst

And I am alone

In a plastic world

Full of thunder and lightning

Heartaches and fears

Sorrow and loneliness

Full of simple-complexities

That cannot be defined.

With one pin prick the bubble burst

But time cannot stand still for me alone.

I must find my own way

Even alone

And see

That I alone have the answers

That can turn my own

Heartache to happiness

Fear to bravery

Sorrow to joy.

UNITY IN DIFFERENTNESS

There is a unity in differentness

Between a man and a woman

    Seed and ground

    Provider and procreator

    Giver and taker.

But this unity occurs

When unlike poles attract—

And in their fusion

There is a continuation of two beginnings,

And as they thrive,

There is a strength that is born

From two opposites,

Equal halves, united, one whole.

AUTUMN ANGER

The seasons change

Red-gold leaves fall

Scattering far and wide

Across a browning landscape

The sun is cool

Just like our cool-stiff words

Peppering each other

With red-hot

Flaming tongues

    Clicking

        Beating

       Out

          Angry retorts.

For like the leaves

    We fall hard

Dancing and writhing in the wind—

    Our cold silences

Cutting

    Like the autumn wind

    Its icy fingers

    Scratching at warm necks

Parched lips

    And watery eyes.

HOW CAN YOU JOKE?

Why do you

Laugh and talk

So glibly?

For I am here

    To finish

    To begin

    To understand

        To learn

            To forget

But you are here

        Just to joke.

WEAKNESSES

You make me angry—

Yet the world does not stand still.

It keeps turning –

And we keep the world turning,

With our consistent-inconsistencies

And our harsh subtleties—

We scream at each other,

Just as others do.

So why should the world stand still

And wait—

For we are not different from all the others

And we all have our weaknesses

So we suffer through our differences

And build shields to protect us from each other

And tongues of swords to strike back

Where the armor has weakened and there are wounds.

Yet our weaknesses are malleable

And our smallest victories are always bittersweet.

TEDDY BEAR

Eyes look straight ahead at some fixed point in space

Reflecting bright light wherever a light source presents.

Nose and Mouth are shaped and etched

with a gentle smile.

So much character manifests in a perfect face

Bright red had and matching scarf

Adorn a round –soft hairy head and almost absent neck

Two outstretched hands are loving points

Ready to hug and yet unable to make contact without help

Two legs, spongy to touch are bent almost backwards

In a comfortable sitting position;

Yes, my warm-soft teddy bear,

You were made to be hugged.

Made to hear me pour out all my secrets,

That I don't want the world outside to know.

You know so much about my comings and goings,

My loves and my hates, my childlike dreams and fears and tears.

You watch over me,

Just like the Angels in heaven do,

With silent contemplation,

Ready when needed,

To comfort in any desperation

Or plight and share in inexplicable joys.

DEFINING MY WORLD

How can I hope to be normal

When I deviate from the norm

When I disagree with common opinion

When I try to change my own world and yours

To suit myself

And damn the world and the norm

Because I want to

Never because I want to do what you want.

The perfect 'I' is strong, willful and everything.

And you are nothing more

Than a significant other

In my world

Where I rule

I matter!

You can be king

But forever must remain in checkmate.

THE VISITOR

So you came—

Finally I've met you:

But did you come to criticize our lives,

Or did you come to see for yourself

What life was like for the others

Out here, so far away

Where home cannot reach us?

We bid you welcome

For with you comes memories of home

The warmth of parents miles away

The discipline of a forgotten tradition

The sadness of timely separation

And the fears and qualms that have laid hidden for so long.

Your candor is appreciated

Yet we hesitate

To change our lives

Just to please you

For when you leave

We must resume our present lives

Knowing that there can be no symbiosis.

Come into our home;

But in leaving, take with you

The things that you see and hear,

The good and bad things that you have perceived

And the secretive happiness and pain

That we can barely hide

In the deep recesses of our hearts.

QUESTIONING LIFE

So many questions

Too many answers

No simple solutions

Life is mathematical

        A complex puzzle

A balancing of inequalities

X is never equal to Y

        And Y is never equal to X

Quantities and Qualities are forever disarrayed—

    Out of balance,

        One against the other.

Thought affects the balancing of the scales,

Time and time again.

The puzzles are never resolved

    Or those that are

        Come full circle

            For further deliberation.

THE PUZZLE

I am yours?

But are you really mine?

Can I dare to hope?

May I dare to wish

that we will grow in love together?

There are questions,

But no answer.

The puzzle has many pieces

But do they fit?

Or are some of the pieces lost forever,

Never to be recovered?

Even with time

Crimes and puzzles may be solved,

So how can I

If I will not wish to wait

Piece together anything as complex as

Two lives?

COMPLAIN

Too much to do

Too little to be

Too much to hear

With everything disagree.

Too much to pay

Too much to buy

Too much to see

And always ask why?

Too much to take

Too little to give

You complain too much

It's just too hard to live!!

Why can't you see

What is wrong with you

You have your faults

Just as others do.

Everything's a farce

Everything's a fade

And you don't much care

When changes are made.

So make up our mind

And do not complain

Then maybe we all

Will be happy again.

MASQUERADE

We all wear masks—

Some are pretty

Some are not.

For we all choose to hide

All we can

From one another—

Behind fitted masks.

Our lives are

Nothing less

Than a masquerade—

Filled to the hilt

With masked-balls

Masked-superficiality

Where no-one ever knows the other

And no one ever will.

ALL I HAVE WANTED

Yes, you cannot understand—

But you are all I have ever wanted

For a long time—

Not school

Not more education

Not more dissent and dissatisfaction with self---

Since my quest for academic perfection

Has led me into a barren wasteland

Where I have lived for nearly a decade.

You are like a camel

Carrying the water of revitalization

Across my waterless wasteland

Into a new and promised land—

Full of new beginnings.

DESPAIR

Why is it that I have these feelings of

    Anger

        Bitterness

            Dissatisfaction

            Despair?

When all I need to do

            Is something quite practical

    Nothing new

        Nothing unique

            Nothing unconventional.

Put my back to the wind

Face the incoming tide

Place my hand on the wheel

Find the money

And sail my boat to the shore.

MODERN SONNET TO AN UNBORN CHILD

Do you feel what I do?

 Child of mine

Do you hear what I hear?

I have waited too long

 To hold you

In the protective circle of my arms

Still you kick and move

Inside of me

Nurtured in quiet softness.

So I must wait impatiently

For God is merciful

You are a precious pearl

Flawless in God's design.

ESSENCE OF LIFE

I do not know you yet

For you are as yet

A living outline

A strong rhythmic heartbeat

A moving squirming mass

A kicking rounded bulge

Of living skin and bone

But I know you hear my voice

And experience the turbulence within me.

I welcome your coming

I welcome your becoming

For you are that

In which the essence of life is embedded—

The beginning in a changing circle.

LIGHTENING

Dropped—

So, you have dropped again

And soon you'll be ready for an impatient world rife with tribulation.

Ready to learn

Ready to experience this life

And take it on, with both hands—

Savoring it,

To make of it what only you can make,

Bringing hope, and joy to a needy world.

Dropped,

Lightening,

Bound for a world with certainty and purpose.

A MESSAGE FOR THE BABY

You sit in your swing

Sometimes sleeping

Sometimes crying

Sometimes smiling—

As of now, winging your way through life—

For you are too small to be concerned

About all of life's problems—

For life to you is but a storm in a tea cup;

And you are too small to know that

This world is what only you can make of it—

And that this world is never aptly

What you would really want it to be.

TO THE LITTLE ONE

Now you are here

And I can't believe it—

You are mine

And his—

And it feels as if I were caught up in a dream—

Like we're still building sand castles

On a deserted beach

        When the tide is out

But then

I hear you

As you cry and fuss

In childish helplessness

        And the dream drifts away

        As the sand castle washes away

        With the incoming tide

For now I realize that

You are ours

Made of the same flesh and bone that we are

And our dream has becomes a reality

For we must begin to rebuild our castle

Once again for you

This time

On solid ground.

WHAT IS THAT SOUND I HEAR?

I hear a sound

And look and look into infinite space—

I stare at everything around me

And hear a rattling sound,

But I don't know where it's coming from.

I grab at and clutch and object

For several seconds

Because it's near to my hand

And I still hear that sound and

I'm sad

Because I can't find out where it's coming from.

I clutch the object again

Put it into my mouth to taste it

And look down at it

And think that maybe

I can have the sound I like

Repeated.

Then maybe I can find it now.

But my hands can't make the object move again—

No—

I don't think that was the sound I heard,

But I think that maybe if I move my hands

The object I am clutching will rattle to my satisfaction—

I don't know yet—

Let's see

Oh there it goes...

Rattle...Rattle...

Oh no...No...! It's falling!

Someone help!!!

Help me explore, I'm only a baby.

THE WAY OF LIFE

You are learning

    Learning about life

    Learning to love life

    Learning to take life as it comes—

With the disappointments and successes

The sad times and the happy times

The good things and the bad things.

But we must teach you

That you'll never get all

That you'll want from life—

For you are fallible

As we are

And you must learn

The best you can

To take the jerks and knocks

Of every day

In your stride.

PACIFIED

Your cries call me to action

For you have once again

Lost your false pacifier we have provided

And you cannot find it on your own.

And I wonder

How you become so pacified and calm—

When a storm is brewing

And turmoil and struggle

Rocks the world so near to you.

For we are not pacified

Finding no solace

In this world of destruction

That you were born into.

SLEEP LITTLE ONE

Sleep little one—

For we are both with you

Guarding you like the guardians of a secret treasure

Hidden from the force of evil

In this miserable world

Protected—

Until you acquire

Protective shields

That when activated—

Stand ready to fend off attack.

You are like a thousand precious gems

Your skills and abilities are dormant

But they will surface and glitter

And sparkle uncut,

Until they are molded, cut and ready

To be inlaid with precious metals

As you attain the highest beauty

Of achievement and promise in this life.

So sleep my little one, sleep.

Sparkle, little jewel, sparkle—

For your well-armed guardians

Await your future with awe.

THOUGHTS IN RETURNING

Mom, Dad

Forgive us—

For we must go back,

And there's no other choice.

We love him—

This man

Who waits,

Patiently,

So far away.

And we need him,

This man,

This foreigner

Whom you don't know

But have talked to

And learnt to respect.

Forgive us Mom, Dad

For all the things

We could not do for you...

For all the things

We could not give to you...

For we are poor,

Not just in pocket,

But also in spirit,

For we need to make our family

One again—

Whole again—

And we cannot look back,

For we have

Made our choice.

THE CLIMB

We do have a future

You and I—

Things look bad right now,

Thing are never simple—

But we do have a future

You and I—

We do.

The future lies at the top

Of a high icy mountain—

And we are still climbing,

Every day we climb---

But we're not experienced climbers—

On a predestined upward path

That we're never ready to climb—

For our footholds often fail.

But experience in climbing

Comes from living

And life is like the fragile ice

On the top of the mountain of predestination—

Where it is warmed by the bright morning sun.

CAPE TOWN STATION

Train doors swing open—

Feet scuffle along the dark muggy platforms

Of Cape Town's suburban station.

Voices rumble, fingers reach

For tickets as corners are rounded.

"Tickets please" the Guard bellows,

"Kaartjies asseblief"…

Feet tread-trample, hands push and shove

In the third class line all the way 'round the corner

The crowd moves forward,

Interspersed,

In, out,

Through inviting openly manned gates

Down

Down endless stairs

Down

Way down into the Golden Acre's

Extravagant display of shop windows and wares;

Where paisley, faceless crowds meander...

In a pickpocket's paradise.

BEHIND MOWBRAY STATION

Crowds waiting

        Forever milling

    People rushing

      Pushing carts

        Carrying bundles

          Running backwards and forwards ---

Bus to train

   Train to taxi

     Bus to taxi

       Car to taxi

         Car to car

           Car to bicycle

Everyone going somewhere under the African sun.

But everyone going nowhere in particular

Just doing the best they can

To make ends meet.

Crowded streets subside

As university buses mowsie down the street

And one taxi after the other

Stops to take on load after load

Of busy passengers

Hanging out of overflowing taxi-cabs

As taxi driver-assistants shout and curse

At all and sundry

While stealthy bicyclers dawdle

In and out

Between

An obscene

Parade of

Walkers

Talkers

Gawkers

Hawkers

    Jaywalkers

Day in and

    Day out

      Living out their lives behind Mowbray Station.

SHOCK REDEFINED: ON THE DEATH OF A FAMILY MEMBER

I look at the letter

News from home

Again and again

It says—

You are dead

You died in your car

You drove into a tree.

I read it again

But it will not ink in

This news

A fuzzy mind

Cannot accept

That you were young

And you are   DEAD

DEAD

i am alive

   i live

     But i could die   too

     Tomorrow!

Why did it happen?

What purpose did your death serve?

Jut pain

That's all

My heart

   Can feel

For our

   Common

    Family

     Distanced

So far away.

PORTRAIT OF ETERNAL YOUTH

You were so young—

When you had a life,

    Chances to be happy

    Chances to make changes

Chances to carve your name into the annals of time.

Your life is over now,

Those chances to do your best

Have all gone.

The future is in your son's hands

A living legacy

In the arms of your mother.

Life was not in vain

For you were and always will be

A portrait of eternal youth.

THE CHAIN IS FOREVER BROKEN

The chain is forever broken

Your death

We must accept

Your mother

And sisters

Must plan

To live

Their lives

Without you.

It's funny

So scary—

Your death.

So final.

I must

I must

Face up

To realities

Too hard

To face

No one

Can live

Forever

For we are born to live

And we are born to die

But through our positivity

Death is but the wilting of a flower

In the vast garden of recreation.

LIFE IS LIKE A TRAIN

Life is like a train

carrying dozens of fares,

to and from unexceptional destinations

as they traverse the rails of life

day in and day out

station for station

concourse to concourse

situation for situation

event to event.

Untiringly, the iron-horse is on time

Its whistle stridently-persistent

Picking up speed

For a long stretch

And then switches tracks

Going quickly on its way

So much the Express train

Passing station for station

While glassy-eyed masses look on,

                As it rushes past unimportant stops

Unstopping

     Uncaring

          In a hurry—

Even when there's one

who misses a stop

     And curses silently

          Under their breath—

Calculating the minutes spent

          On a long walk back.

This train is ardent—

Carrying boarded passengers smartly on,

Forward,

     Onward

To their destinations

And beyond.

A stop is made in-between stations

As impatient time-watchers look on—

Talking excitedly

Into their mobile phones

As time moves sluggishly on—

Making feverish promises

Again revisited and revised

Once the train slows

Or the doors reopen

On an unanticipated-gapping platform.

Then the train jerks

Violently to a start

And begins to move

Bodies moving in unison

At attention—

Their movements uncurbed,

As the wind is knocked out

Of a large personage

With a wide bola hat

And a grey summer suit

Who falls against another

As impatient hands push back

Disengages him sideways

With a coarse expletive—

Yet the train moves

Stealthily on

Like a cheetah

Reaching the kill

Sleek and efficient

Running silent footedly

Into the station

As the doors open wide

Like the cheetah's jaws,

Latching onto the kill

As umpteen stragglers

Make a fast escape

Down a dingy platform

With thousands of vacant eyes

Fastened on their backs

Every one

Watching and waiting

For their turn to exit

With grace and aplomb.

ABOUT THE AUTHOR

Gloria Creed-Dikeogu is the Director of an academic library in Kansas, and divides her free time between working part-time in a public library setting and teaching Business courses as an adjunct. She was born in Cape Town, South Africa, worked as a public librarian and later taught high school English until age 26, when she came to Kansas as a graduate student. Gloria lives with her husband and son in Lawrence, Kansas.

38648462R00067

Made in the USA
Charleston, SC
11 February 2015